Ice Maidens

Ice Maidens

Edmund Cusick

HEADLAND

First published in 2006
by
HEADLAND PUBLICATIONS
38 York Avenue
West Kirby, Wirral
CH48 3JF

British Library Cataloguing in Publication Data.
A full CIP record for this book is available from the British Library
ISBN
1 902096 94 0

Printed in Great Britain by
L. Cocker Ltd.
Unit A9, Prospect Street, Liverpool L6 1AU

HEADLAND acknowledges the financial
assistance of Arts Council England

ARTS COUNCIL ENGLAND

For a Foxy Lady

Acknowledgments

Some of these poems have appeared in the following magazines: *Avalon Magazine, Broom Cupboard, Poetry Wales, The New Writer;* and in the anthologies *Poetry Pool, Poetry Pool 2, Poetry Pool 3, Poet's England, Volume 22: Wirral* and *The Poet's View: Poems for Paintings in the Walker Art Gallery* (ed. Gladys Mary Coles).

'Pwyll' first appeared in *Gronw's Stone: Voices from the Mabinogion* (Headland, 1998) and 'Devon Churches' in *The Writer's Workbook* (Arnold, 2000).

Other poems have been prizewinners or shortlisted in the following competitions: Aberystwyth (University of Wales), Blue Nose, Bridport, Borderlines, First Thursday, the Housman Society, the Keats-Shelley Memorial Society, the Kent and Sussex, Lancaster Litfest, the Library of Avalon, Llandudno Festival, Lit Up, Mere Poets, Poetry Life, Poetry London, Poetry Now, Trewithen, Ver Poets, Ware Poets.

I am grateful to many whose inspiration and assistance has helped me on the long road to completing this collection: notably Stella Shakerchi, Rose Flint, Lindsay Clarke, and to all those at Liverpool John Moores University and elsewhere who have offered support, both practical and spiritual, through the years. I owe a particular debt to Ann Gray for her unfailing understanding and advice.

Especial thanks are due to Gladys Mary Coles, without whose aid and encouragement, this collection would not have been compiled.

The front cover reproduction of a detail from John William Waterhouse's *Hylas and the Nymphs* is by courtesy of Manchester Art Gallery.

CONTENTS

Lipstick	11
Conjuration	12
Despatch from the Slush Pile	13
Aubade	14
Devon Churches	16
St Martin's, Laugharne	17
Year of Grace	18
Kelpie	19
Waterhouse	20
At Vindolanda	21
Norham Gardens	23
Strix	24
May 2012	25
Nana	26
Nimue	27
Pwyll	28
Morgana	29
On Call	30
The Girls on my Corridor	31
Making Love	33
Her question	34
Oviedo	35
Lindisfarne	36
Lent	37
Reading Your Lips	38
Good Friday	39
Coming Home	40
Ariadne	41
The Fitting	42

CONTENTS (continued)

You know I said I was a model . . .? 43
The Following Foods Are All Rich In Zinc 44
At Our Lady Hospital 46
Rapid Response 48
City Pride 50
Matt 52
66° North 54
Igor 55
Ny Alesund 56
Polar Hotel 58
Ytrenorskoya 60
Life Long Learning 61
Jill 63
Lorrayne 64
Can I help you? 66
Mistress Tanya 67
Speaking in Tongues 69
Bianca 71
Homecoming 73
Coed y Farden 74
January 77

Lipstick

You're gone, but still I feel the kiss
you left me with. Its numb taste
teases out of memory things I've buried:
make up and make believe,
dressing up, a face smudged
with powder in my mother's compact,
the scarlet rising in my fingers,
shameless; *Rocky Horror* nights,
a girl, her tongue-tip squeezed
with concentration, commanding
me to pout, smudging my mouth
hard, tissues in a red nailed hand,
the soft assault of lipstick, the shock
of my own mascaraed eyes.

Conjuration

This the simplest of all sorceries:
a circle cast in sand, the long vigil
to the dawn. Four elements conjoin:

sea weed and wet wood twist in the flame.
Demons of air and water rise now
in spume, answering to thought,

and in the boom and flicker of the surf
water transmutes to light.
Across these embers as stars fade

the work is done, and we commune
with elementals whose eyes disclose
hunger of fire, harshness of sand.

Till when gull-light comes, the waves
recede: the spell complete.

Despatch from the Slush Pile

Not an easy posting. It's hard
to settle in at first, difficult
to make friends. Most people here
are prostitutes or tramps, or young men,
lonely, misunderstood. Everyone
is Scorpio or Gemini.
There are the odd local customs
to get used to: skirts perpetually slide back,
revealing stockinged thighs; labia
are by convention moist, nipples
and penises erect. And etiquette:
husbands must arrive early
and unexpected. At night I am obliged
to squint through the blinds and watch
the couplings of my neighbours.

The economy is in rough shape,
being dependent on the manufacture
of adjectives, lately in surplus. But some rules
are rigidly enforced: clubs
must be seedy, cups cracked, fat men
required to leer. Punctuation is in short
supply except for exclamation marks!
At least, though, every citizen
has a word processor. I miss
the usual things: gardens, clean
clothes, conversation. One does
one's best. Sometimes, though it's hardly
worth mentioning, I find I am writing -
just for myself, of course.

Aubade

Tonight I am driving you back
to be with your real dad for the New Year.
Parker at your service, Lady Penelope.
You roll your eyes. *Whatever.*
You lie on the back seat, long legs bent
under swathes of duvet, your face
candy striped in the orange play of streetlamps,
the skin inside your wrist so white that, when
we stop, it takes the faintest sheen
of red, then green.
If I could drive you anywhere,
where would it be? *Florida.*
In Britain? *Whatever . . . You choose*

I watch you in the mirror, stretching
the seat-belt's tense embrace, tangling
headphones in your hair. Your eyes are closed
before I reach the empty motorway, slip
into that alien country that is the last night
of the year. Tonight there are no police,
no trucks, no roadworks, only
a scattering of fugitive cars, cats' eyes
streaming like tracer and once the splash
of rockets in amethyst and gold.

You're restless in your sleep, your feet
kicking my back as Sailing By begins.
M5 THE SOUTHWEST. There's time
tonight for three hundred miles
before the dawn; enough to reach

Cornwall and the Lizard, Goonhilly,
its barbed wire glittering with ice,
the scarlet pulse of warning beacons;
time, as night thins to grey, to reach
the silent square where fog condenses
on rusting postcard racks and ice cream signs;

Cornish Gems, its window hushed
with velvet boxes promising
serpentine and iron pyrites; time

to reach the cove before the sun
flares pink through winter mist, to stop
and wind the window to the lash of spray,
the numb kiss of salt, to watch,
as the car grows cold, the waves,
your eyes' first flicker.

Devon Churches

You keep looking for it, a place so still
that, after the door's echo, you can hear
a lark, a tractor fields away, aisles filled
with the cold quiet shock of others' prayer:
that pause. The saints in the late August
sun bleeding scarlet stains across the face
of an unplastered wall, the soft white hush
of dying lilies. As though some other place
were near, held between breaths, as, in the glass
Adam is held in the red clench of scales;
as though in the damp book you'd find, at last
a cryptic hint of some elusive grail,
the confirmation of this search: some guide,
some word or name, a sign you recognise.

St Martin's, Laugharne

A strange find. The church dappled
by passing shadow and quick light. Within,
this image, in glass now brilliant in the sun,
a scarlet serpent coiled around a tree,
the woman and the man as pale as angels,
the tree of close stitched leaves, flaming
with Eden's emerald. And in this moment
the serpent burning holy, the apple perfect.
No sin. The image seems to breathe in stillness,
ebbing with the shift of light and branch.
This smell of churches: a faith grown musty
in religious damp. But imagine - to kneel
here, and taste redemption in the fruit
that stings the tongue with sweetness,
beneath this mystery: God in his first flesh
succumbing; Satan exalted in the tree.

Year of Grace

That was the year the leopards came.
No one believed it. Shadows slinking
under hedgerows, eyes
disputed in the headlights. In the morning
fleeces, bones, stripped of meat.

It was said extremists had let
them loose. They had escaped
from privatised menageries.
They had come because we had made
a land fit for leopards.

Some went with rifles into the dark,
and some of these returned.
In barbarous regions
it was reported there were women
who took beasts' shapes
at the dark of the moon.
Some were burned.

Prophets came, thin and fluent,
preaching from Revelations.
The church counselled tolerance,
and to keep children away
from wooded areas.

Now we farm carefully, yielding them
their tithe of land, hearing at night
their passions. We admire the country stars
no longer. The new road signs
DANGER WILD ANIMALS
are fading, seem natural.

Kelpie

From the painting by Herbert Draper

Some words do not translate, do not exist
in English. One tongue slips through the other`s grasp,
ignoring our clear divisions of green
from blue, blue from grey. Hidden
in the Gaelic are other hues, shades
we do not see. In the Gaeltacht the light
refracts anew, the boundaries of the visible
and the invisible are different: the blind
have been seers; sight defies the eyes.

He, a painter in this alien spectrum, learned this.
Drawn from his familiar colours into light
broken and rewoven, his eyes ceased
to resist: he crossed that rift in subtle sense
which holds the worlds apart and keeps us sane.

Faithful, he painted what he saw,
what could not be there. At the pool of Glas Allt
an elemental spirit watching by the water,
Kelpie, knowing the word true.

Waterhouse

Beneath the water's face he finds
in these green depths the soul refracts
like light, sees in his rippling eyes
the world within, self upon bright self
breaking to his sight. So the artist
turns from love to the lure of water
and illusion, the gaze of painted
creatures meeting his own gaze.

The women he desires he bathes
in this same stream, flowing
from canvas to canvas, making
of them mermaids, sirens. They gleam
between tall reeds, milk-white naiads
playing among the waterlilies,
dragonflies. Imploring pools lap
at their childs' breasts. Just once,

as Hylas, he came to the brink
of caressing these pink-nippled
girls, the nymphs he thirsted for.
Yet as their hands, cold as river
pearls, reached to draw him
down, he knew some colours
move only in water, are seen
only by those who drown.

At Vindolanda

floods spill through tarpaulin shrouds, burst
over lawns and paths. Oaks bend
before storm water's weight. Three girls run across the ruins,
feet sodden, their faces masked and glinting
in clear plastic macs, pearl eyed
with rain. Exhumed from these earthworks
the first letter between women, its cursive script
stripped from centuries of mud's discretion: *I offer*
prayers for you, Lavinia, at the temple of the nymphs.

All along the wall, each mile fort has its shrine,
each villa a sacred well: the legions surrendering
to the cold communion of the springs, drinking
in the lapping voices of outlandish spirits,
till every river's name invokes a Goddess.

The girls twirl in a swirling hail, hold up
cupped hands, squeeze under ropes, splash
in the open dig. Their plebeian feet
churn the quarters of centurions and priests.
The sky falls, whirling down to three wide open
mouths. Prised from fresh dredged graves,
the statues are paraded under hot museum lights:
Local Deities, Water Spirits, Nymphs of the Springs.
Between this water and the sculpted stones,
some living thing that we have lost. But here,
in Vindolanda among the nymphs,
I remember how on the frontier

of sleep you came to me, night by night, holding me
breathless, appearing then as you were, once,
in the azure glare of underwater lights: the crossed straps
scarring your pale shoulders; the wet veil of hair
slashed across one cheek; tight drops
scaling your tensed thighs, reptilian,
beautiful; the cup of shadow offered
at the hollow of your collar bone; you,
balanced, as herons balance on the brink

of killing. Or some discarnate thing,
which, as you dived, you yielded to,
till your blue nails tore the water's skin,
splayed across the tiles; and after them your face
rising, broken and baptised
in the mosaic flickering of light.

My clothes are a shell of water.
There is no one here, no-one but the three girls,
splashing, unafraid; above, the pregnant clouds,
piling and coiling, murmuring in the soft breath
of gods that is like the sound of boulders
falling. The tarpaulins stretch
to bulging pouches, growing.

Norham Gardens

In this room measure the hours,
the seasons, by light and birdsong only,
by the triple bark of foxes
in the dark, the fresh wet roses
cut for Mary's Day.

This room, made empty to the south
fills with the rising moon
holds silence as a breath
waits for the coming of its Christ.

Strix

Home again, and sleepless, a cry outside
comes like a memory. As children
we would wake in the illicit hours, lie rapt
in the night that vibrated on two cold notes:
owl call and silence. Older, we ventured
to the trees, strained our throats to answer,
our rough owl words half way to witchcraft.
So all have conjured syllables of your tongue
to cast your name. Saxons called you *ule*,
Normans, *hulet*; monks, hearing your scream
scored through their vigils, transcribed
the consonants like claws: *strix*.

May 2012

Four days of madness.Thanks to CNN, everyone remembers
the same things: post boxes tarted up in ten mismatching hues
of blue emulsion; the sombre thuds of mutinous howitzers
saluting from the Mound; the MI5 expulsions; the killing
made by Edinburgh's wide boys in panic selling
the night the pound was ditched; customs checks on the M6;
the English crowding Gretna Green to feel the pricks
of thistled Euros on their virgin palms; the protest from the Queen.

We missed all that: adrift six miles outside the shipping lanes,
radio and rudder out. What I remember now's the Frigate
Hurta from the Northern Isles, turning, shuddering
alongside, the wind, slapping out the Saltire at her stern,
whipping up her wake in sudden flurries; that moment's calm,
the sandy-haired lieutenant calling down *nae worries.*

Nana

A farm, pitched like a ship
against the hail of seaspray on cliffs
eaten year by year by the malicious tide.
Upstairs, one bedroom wall is window,
a slow hour glass filling with the sea.
And at this rising, sinking line
Nana, a hundred years dead
and nine years old, kneels to stare,
measuring endlessly time she cannot feel.

All who have come here, gazed
on this bleak shore have sensed it,
that line of ending, ebbing and drawing near.
Here, men dug with their own hands,
the bones of deer, raised stone slabs
above their dead, slanted to the setting sun.
The Celts called these bruised, weed-stained
reefs Caer Arionrhod, poised between life and life,
death and death. Here the knell of Christ
tolled to mark the road to the isle of pilgrims,
where the brown limbs of saints are laid,
thick as apple roots beneath the spade.

So at my own death, I may recall
these fields with their rusting fence,
this tattered swell that weeps and fills, these deeps
where time is held in store among the waves.
Once more then, perhaps, I'll see her, her image
flat against the patient light: Nana,
still watching, waiting, for that final bell
to wake her into freedom, into sleep.

Nimue

And when he left her she climbed the cliffs
of serpentine and granite, found
the secret place where adders sun themselves,
cross hatched with menace and allure, snake
upon snake basking in glistening coils.
She lay among them in the hot breath
of thyme and samphire, slept. As she dreamed
she heard the swift burst of the surf, felt the heat
of rock beneath her, the sun's heat
on her back and still another flame
as though not just the sun had scorched her,
but, added to its strength, the red fires
of Aldebaran and Antares, Draco and Serpens,
rising from the dark of summer stars.
When she woke she watched the waves
writhe their rippled backs into the strand.
In the evening she rose to face a scarlet sun,
holding his heat within her; waited, silent,
at the chapel in the cove among the wives
of fishermen; ate the thin wafer
from the priest's cold hand.

Pwyll

Nothing may I take from you
whom I have lain by for a year,
not even your leave.
Behind my eyelids, I see ivory hounds
gleaming around the stag I brought to bay,
my own dogs shivering.
That night I came to you, dressed
in your husband's flesh, your skin
was blue-white as his hounds, your body
wet as snow for me, your touch eager, burning
like ice that steals the blood heat from the mouth.
Something held me back, though you were willing,
that night, and each night since. It was not fear,
nor yet honour for he whose place I took.
I wished, perhaps, to keep one deed untrespassed,
desiring, but not wanting, this last communion,
knowing I would care for no mortal woman
after you. And it is so.
You do not know me, trapped
behind your master's eyes, guess only disdain
as I turn my face to the wall.
Each night I hear desire
and pride wrestle in your breathing;
after that, despair.
The sun's warmth strokes your hair, embraces you.
Before night falls I will hunger for you,
wish I had been
less pure.

Morgana

We will inherit that land of poppies, pomegranates
the bright isle which drowning men have seen
as the last darkness parts before their sight,
which rests, they say, beyond the furthest west,
but lies, in truth, beyond the stark horizon
at every compass point; to which the soul must turn,
quivering to stillness.

And while from that glittering sea we turn our eyes
it sends its signs to us: the hush
after birdsong in the dusk, the red sun
sinking beneath the earth, and at the mass,
looking from face to face, we see its light there,
as each sips the blood of the eternal kingdom.

Apples, and apple wine, brewed sharp and sweet
as the serpent`s kiss, scents of cinammon and clove
twine round the trees of those green glades
where we will meet again with those we loved,
and know them beautiful, as in their youth,
or in the hour when they were most themselves.

On Call

He came in leaning on her, his chest
streaked with stains, his mouth open,
saying, *I'll be alright*. Probing his hair
I saw blood breaking, clotting
on the scalp. While she sat still he rambled
pleading to friends who offered
a range of stories: a wall, a lamp-post,
an unlucky fall. He rolled his head:
This shirt, it's ruined. My best shirt.

And what comes back, returning
to an empty bed, is not that wound,
but her tight thighs as I knelt by him
the finger clenched between her teeth,
her widened eyes, her hand touching him
as I have not been touched.

The Girls on my Corridor

are having their night out. The walls
above the bath still flush their heat;
tiles stream their blend of sweats.
The taps are smothered, muffed
with strangled tights. From open caps
their bottles leak shampoo and body
scrub, slide fingers of warm gel
down the enamel. Each has her own taste:
peach, strawberry, orange, grape.
As I grope for tongues of soap
bright smears of passion fruit
rub me in golden showers.

Beyond the swollen door, they're singing
fit to bust, bawling out flat choruses
and whoops -they're going to live
forever: squeezing smooth hips
into split skirts, trying ruthless haltertops
for size, squirting in-your-face
perfume at thirsty cleavage, draining
helpless necks of strawberry Hooch,
their cheeks sprayed by the starry pricks
of glitter dust that constellate
the rising signs of lust.
Then come the desperate horns
of waiting cabs, the expert rhythm
of their Friday heels: they're gone.

I'm left with this: the flashing pulse
of strip light, two razors, their choked
slits gagging, stuffed with secret fur,
one bleached blonde hair stuck to my leg,
wet patches slapping on the floor,
the damp passage reeking
of deodorant and talc. To bed.

Five hours and they'll be coming,
shrieking, back to give me lip.
Some of us have got to sleep,
you know. *Yeh, right, you tosser.*
Enjoy yourself! The bangs and howls
as at last they pull triumphant doors.
Have one on us!
and then the squeals, commands,
obscenities in Barnsley vowels.

In the gloom of daylight,
after haggard lads have stumbled
to the loo, made their escapes,
they're up, shuffling in padded socks
from bed to bed, their faces freckled
with angelic pox, clutching dirty cups
of last night's cider, sucking hunks
of toast and chocolate spread. *Hiya!*
they shout. *Hope we didn't get you up?*

Making Love

Upstairs they're doing it
again. The steady creaks
remorseless, it goes on
for hours. Down here
each smile is measured,
deliberate. Her hands
by her side, her eyes tired
with repulsed hints.
The playfulness he loved
in her has gone. She makes
no advances now. Instead
they watch TV, drowning
out the noise, hoping
for a way out. The telephone
perhaps, anything.

Her question

startles him. Each way his thoughts run,
he cannot hide, cannot *not think*:
the waitress staying after hours for one
last order, the librarian in her high heels
stamping her authority, the WPC who pulls him
over, the surly pharmacist in her white coat
prescribing pain. How to penetrate the ways
of the imagination? He looks
away. *I don't have fantasies* he says.

Oviedo

Fiesta. In the hotel, one attic room
was left. Among madonnas, candles,
lamps, a handle in a wall of glass
opened to my key, and, through the looking glass,
a loft where a century's self-doubt
lined slanted walls. As though it were a sin
to cast away a mirror or a saint:
they had this place. Their angled gaze
crossed and double-crossed, framing
each other into infinity, stretching
further than my eyes dared. Then you came there.

As we touched, I watched my hands caress
the hair of one whose face was hidden,
betraying you with her, but we moved together
to see our twins in those other silvered rooms
break their incestuous embrace to gaze at us
wide-eyed. Their startled smiles made us
smile, till they, as we, turned to kiss.

That night I woke on a double bed, in the cold calm
of mirrors, found us back to back, like children
joined at the spine, your foot's sole pressed
to mine, the heart's symmetry written in our flesh.

Lindisfarne

Evensong is said slowly here. My responses
stumble over unaccustomed pauses, trespassing
into silence. Time is different, months marked
by the flicker of flowers on sand, centuries
by the weathering of script on stone. All
infused with ritual, the liturgy of that bare mass
served by the elements, in which the tide
is heartbeat, and the gulls scream antiphon.

Each day, salt water is blessed and broken
on the white table of the land.
All becomes epiphany: a church
encircled by the sea, crowded
with silence; poppies bleached thin
as insects' wings; walls transfigured

to poems of stone. Here prayers
rise, merciless as thorn.

Lent

Now is the time of miracle.
In his mercy he forbids us meat,
yet for these forty days he veils
the pious vigilance of the saints
and from our fallen eyes unpeels
the blinding scales of reason.

Now we understand that coneys
are clean of all the taint of flesh,
being, indeed, vegetable, and watch
at dusk their soulless forms pour back
into the earth. For forty days we eat them,
sowing their bones around our fields;
see them spring up from the wet ground,
shaking clean their fur from coats
of soil, blinking their newborn
eyes like pebbles.

By the act and ash of faith, we see
the world anew: children playing
at the shore cut their feet on razored
bills of sea geese growing
in the pools. From clasped beds of beaks
we see their webbed feet fan
in unison, waiting the dark moon
when they will break the surface,
preen their feathers, supple, smooth
as sealskin, swim to our waiting nets.

This grace for forty days: we see
how all creation is malleable
as clay. The abbot summons lizards
from cucumbers, lamb from compliant
turnip, quail from mute mushrooms,
their hearts shaped from yew berries.
Then, reluctant, wise, he puts us from him,
banishes us again to worldly sense.

Reading Your Lips

Your timing perfect, you have slipped
to the ladies, leaving me poised
between coffee and dessert, fantasy
and fulfilment. So I hold the long handled
spoon you held, an inch from your lipstick,
as you spoke, paused, almost embraced
the heaped mound of cream, ice cream,
hot chocolate fudge, then waited,
and spoke again, hesitated, opened to take it -
and again delayed, tormenting me until
I took it from you, guided it between
your opened lips, felt it press the soft
flesh within, your tongue teasing
and releasing a mouthful of pleasure,
then as I withdrew, the soft, slight
tug as your lips pouted to suck
it clean. I do not know if, after this,
we will go home together.
It no longer matters.

Reenactment of feeding someone very personal & affectionate

rich poisions. over stating

attention to desert & the mouth.

Sexual poem. full of desire.

- imagery
- form
- line length
- Rhythm
- Tempo.
- concencious
- Anima
-

Good Friday

She enters. Her heels rap the marble floor.
Her coat sweeps her ankles.
Above, a flood of leaded darkness
presses the outlines of the saints.

Charcoal flickers scarlet on the altar.
We gather at the rail.
The priest pushes five brass daggers
into the candle's yielding wax.

We sing. We breathe in incense, dizzy.
We summon into the candlelight
the lamb crucified, a severed ear, a kiss.
Somewhere a wound is pierced.

We kneel. She takes the silver chalice
in gloved palms, inclines her head,
drinks, wipes the rim clean
of lipstick, holy blood. We rise,

embrace, her fingers sheathed
in leather, her upturned collar
brushing my cheek, her breath
a psalm of scent and wine.

Coming Home

early he found her
sitting bare-legged
by the open drawer,
the folder he'd taped
shut. Around her, magazines,
photographs, of other
women's feet, stilettoes
draped in gleaming
chain, a catalogue:

ankle boot w/ padlock fastener
courts, black patent, w/ studded ankle strap
gibson slingback, 6 inch heel
zip-sided thigh-boot, vinyl, available bl / r

'I'm size four' she said.

Ariadne

The stories lied, of course.
It was not wool she used
to guide him through the labyrinth
of his desires, but something finer,
bought with premonitory pain.

Now on my crumpled pillow I find
the threads you left behind, and wind
them round my wrist, tight enough
to cut, just as you'd wish.

The Fitting

It rained, and you needed new shoes.
In Frayne's, I knelt at your feet,
took your trainers in my hand,
and slid them free, unwrapped
from a rustle of white tissue
the high black boots, polished
to a sheen, smelling of soft leather,
secrets. Took your stockinged feet,
eased them in, then threaded, hook
by bright steel hook, crossing and pulling
hard, till the thin cords cut
my fingers, the leather squeaking tight,
laced you to the knee, and tied
the knots, while you laid
your gloved hand on my hair.

And as you paced the carpet, you looked
back, for my approval,
as though it could be denied.

You know I said I was a model . . .?

It's just that I'd imagined *Vogue* or *Elle;*
though *Countess Vixen* is quite upper crust:
the leather corset squeezing out your bust,
the rusty chains and racks, the torture cells
disturbingly convincing - cobwebs, dust,
all real, the man trussed firmly at your heel
looking half-concussed, who's bound to kneel
to worship the stilettoes which you thrust
towards his eager tongue with such disgust.
You've got men sussed: those who long for pain,
frustrated and afraid, the secret slaves
who must serve a cruel Mistress to be saved.
'*It's not just lust* -' I feel, as you explain,
your hand restrain my wrist '- *It's about trust* . .'

The Following Foods Are All Rich In Zinc

Day one. In the park the ponds slop thick
with spawn. Small girls in wellies
scoop it up in cloudy jars, wipe clinging
strings of gel from slimy fingers.

Relax. A holiday,
some vitamins, perhaps.

Day two. The supermarket swarms with baby dinners,
toy spaghetti. In *Seasonal Goods,* Mother's Day bouquets
give way to eggs and bunnies, bubble-wrapped.

Loose underpants. Fresh orange juice.

Day ten. A day of obligation. Tonight I kneel
in a cold bath and splash
my shrinking balls to penitent bruises.

Every other night, or every night
if you can manage, especially
from day eleven. Eat oily fish.

Month two. *Your count is fine*,
the blonde technician says,
looking at the desk. *But they're not swimming*
quite as well as we would like.
Are you taking any prescribed drugs?
In the Thames the trout are turning female,
dissolving in a tide of oestrogen.

Herbal remedies, Tai Chi. No evidence exists

Month nine. Every second Christmas
card disgorges happy news: pudgy
photographs, huge eyes. They share
a common look: mocking, smug.

Have you thought of donors? We import
from Scandinavia, where there is a surplus.
The most stringent tests. If you change
your mind? There is a waiting list, that’s all.

Month twelve. The park again. A mother
pulls her twins away from me.
The frogs are back, the water
lumpy, glistening like eyes.

At Our Lady Hospital

In the porch the Blessed Virgin's mounted,
life size, half way up the wall. Her palms
are pressed in prayer, porcelain lips pursed
tight, smooth cheeks stung pink with rapture.
Under her satin robe, chaste plaster breasts
swell to feed the God who grows in her. Neck,
face, feet are naked. Her bare soles trample
the snaking stems of roses; slim toes
anointed in a flood of perfume
crushed from their swollen heads.

I'm here to masturbate. Nuns and nurses
whisper past, stockinged, veiled. Blowdried
receptionists, immaculate in matching tops, lay
fountain pens to glossy lips, smile identically
to the laboratory. *Don't worry,*
the technician says, *you won't be disturbed.*
The loo is airless, close. Through a little grille
voices talk of purities and blood. Quiet, I ease out
from my bag the mag: open it at Liz
from Norwich, hefting her huge breasts
like half ripe grapefruit. *I'd like to get*
three men in me at once. Longsuffering,
she parts her labia like a wound.
Behind her head a goldfish bowl
catches the light. The fish floats limp. No joy

Five minutes gone, I'm flogging
a dead horse; the jar's lewd mouth is huge
enough to swallow cupfuls. Leafing on, I find
Angela, goddess in black rubber mask, spiked
heels, padlocked collar with studded
crucifix, demanding worship: *I like*
to walk all over men. Her skin
is white as lilies, her nipples sharp
as thorns. At last it comes,
scourging into pain: a single smear.

The lab technician collects my offering,
eyes his watch, nods paternally. My shirt
hangs wet with sweat. *It's hard,* he says,
when you're under pressure. The twins
avert their eyes from my flushed face.
Outside rose petals strew the drive;
the cold wind's like a grace.
Looking back, the virgin smiles,
inscrutable, a calm like absolution.

Rapid Response

That summer, he passed the warm nights
listening to Police landrovers hum down
his street, the screams of sirens, hot-wired
cars. On the radio, drug feuds, turf wars,
the latest shooting. By day, streets swarmed
with breasts in printed T shirts
Too Hot to Handle; Sex Kitten;
All This and Brains Too. Saturdays, he'd watch
the girls in Paradise Street, languid as hot-house flowers
beneath the bus station's circling flies,
and hover there, daring the sting
of point blank glares: *My Place Now*
You Should Be So Lucky. And ambushing
him round corners on the Aigburth Road,
thin-faced gangs of girls, thirteen,
fourteen, in shiny boots, bootleg *CK*,
Use me Abuse me; Drop Dead Gorgeous.

All that summer there was only one
who triggered a response in him, the one he saw
that afternoon, not eating ice-cream.
The bulky men around her licking
double cones, white smears
on their uniforms, joking in the brutal
sun as if they had all afternoon
to kill. She, bent to the wing mirror
of the Mr.Whippy, her ash blonde pony tail
pushed through the chequered cap, reflected
eyes clocking him, just once. She gleamed
with polished leather, ammunition, cuffs.
Her fingers concentrated on the cylinder
of lipstick, the angle awkward,
body armour crushing her breasts.
Getting it right. And haltered round her neck
the squat machine-gun, Heckler and Koch.

Later he heard the brakes, the neighbour's dog,
was there before they got the cordon up,
amongst the mess of headlights, the trollies
with their darkening sheets, the escort's body
honeycombed with wide eyed holes,
the windscreen spiderwebbed. He saw her,
heaving off the vest, wiping her face
dragging out the bobble from her hair,
the white blouse stretched and damp
with sweat, a hint of lace beneath.

That night he lay under his window, opened
to the small rasp and whir of moths,
the brush and shiver of insects on his arms.
Imagined her, choosing her position,
her practiced hands judging
the moment, that squeeze
of pressure: making it count.

City Pride

I've one hand on her breast,
the other at her throat. She's legless, limp.
Give her one more try. Her skin
is smooth and dry; her thin lips
taste of antiseptic, rubber, the last man
to do this to her. No response. *Next One.*

Her mouth exhales my breath at once,
a short, frustrated sigh. We try her now
in turns, each fumbling for
a rhythm, groping for the point where blood
will answer to two fingers. No joy.

Back to my seat. The windows frame a rash
of slime around a roof's charred ribs,
a bricked-up church, a concrete void, choked
with mattresses and tyres. At Jay's Medical,
winner of a City Pride award, the unemployed
are taught *First Aid at Work*. Here we learn
of shock and burns, the risk of heart attack,
to search in pockets, check for exit wounds,
listen for the crunch of bones. At lunch
the huge ex-welder, corseted, once of Camell Laird
comes back with battered cod and chips, Bensons
to replace the ones he's shared, two
cans of stout, the *Echo*: SHOTGUN HORROR
IN CITY TAKEAWAY. The white fish-spine
protrudes through bloodless flesh
in complicated fractures. Our instructor, Mick,
ex-ambulance, eats clumsy home-made
sandwiches, consoles his doll, tells us,
as he gently rubs her down, about the Trust
that laid him off, its new brand uniforms,
and the man who walked three hundred yards,
holding his severed arm. His shirt has week-old stains.

Last, we get a chance to buy, discounted,
first aid kits with latex gloves, lip shields
in case of HIV, a badge.
Mick leaves with his girl, zipped
in half a body bag, cradled to his chest.
He lays her in the boot; awkward, sad,
as though she was his first, or last.
Take you home now, Pat, he says.

Matt

Got him. Matt cuts the engines. As we drift
he climbs the cabin roof, balanced, easy,
in the lurch of swell. His eyes lift a single fin
from miles of sea we've tried to search.
He points. *There. He's diving. Six minutes.*
Propellors gurgle as we turn. He's stalking it,
forty metres down. We hold our breath.
A chain clinks on the mast. Five minutes.
We whisper, as though afraid our words
could sound down twenty fathoms
and then it blows, near enough to touch,
its skin as smooth as tight stretched silk.
An eye, a ragged scar along a fin.
Orca, Matt says. *Attack anything.*
Seals, porpoise. No discrimination.

At night they're diving in a green half light.
Matt checks them, man by man, buckled,
strapped, into depth guage, air tank, knife.
As they ready for the jump he puts his hand
on each man's shoulder, once. The masks
they turn to him fill with his own image,
then bow to darkness, silt. We wait.

On the deck where everything makes noise
he comes behind me, silent as the air.
Ashore, he never seems to follow me,
but always to be there. It's like a private game.

In one cold hour they're back; surface
in a swirl of bubbles, struggle at the ladder,
their own mass too burdensome to raise.
Matt lifts them with one hand, tears
their faces from rubber balaclavas.

Now, leaning at the rail alone, we stare
into the slow half-trance of signal buoys
and beacons, hear the slap of the Atlantic,
watch stars dance above St Agnes.
There's questions I don't ask. He gives no regiment,
no dates. He talks of Wilfred Owen, of lost mates,
of getting off his face and waking on the beach,
watching the dawn. He mutters once, *The Army let me do*
what I was good at. But it's late, the whisky's
low, before he says, *I didn't have a problem*
killing people - it was other things,
that made me leave. His face is sealed,
remote and tight, when he says to the lights,
the sea, not me, *The Army*
made me do what I was good at.

66° North

I almost missed them, their sombre trucks
pulled off the road, my eyes
dulled from eight hundred kilometers
of stunted birches, lakes, bog,
only the dashboard clock dividing
white nights from days.
NORDKAPP 250km
MURMANSK 320Km
Every hour a steeple, a huddle
of concrete houses, a stack of oil drums
wooden huts on stilts.

There were villages here, once, every twenty,
thirty kilometers. As they retreated
the Vermacht burned everything
churches, houses, towns.
They brought a word for this
from the Ukraine, from Byelorussia:
in English you say scorched earth.

But here they were, strung across
the featureless terrain, surveying
nothing. Mapping the arctic circle, reservists
in olive green fatigues; a sergeant
in winter warfare uniform, jagged zebra-patterns
of taiga in snow. And a third, with gentle eyes,
slim hands, his hooded cape paintball-splashed
with pinks, violets, saffron, the sort of camouflage
a boy could wear at carnival.
It is for snipers. In the spring
the tundra is covered with flowers.

I shared brandy with them, watched them
measuring the earth in perfect English.
Each year it moves South, a kilometer
or so, then some years, North again-

drove on into unending sunset.
But I still see him, as I sleep,
a marksman with magenta eyes,
rising from a field of purple saxifrage,
his rifle barrel draped with childhood colours,
his face a mask of flowers.

Igor

shrugs, lifts a single finger, contemptuous.
Eskimos? In Russian there is one word
for snow, schoolteacher. This -
He jerks a thumb at the fields of drift ice,
its grey redeemed only by the distant yellow
excrement of walrus, the red-brown excrement
of seals, at pyramids, arches, thrown up
by chance collisions of floe on floe. On the port bow,
an aquamarine cathedral, glistening,
tortured into spires. *It is ice, yes ?*
Why do you want more words?

On Igor's watch, while the crew sleeps
in endless light, between SatNav, radar,
radio, the log, he teaches me fragments
of latitude, depth charts, the sea.

Half my age, he commands
ice strengthened vessel *Akademic Kaplinsky,*
registered Murmansk, bends course to chase
whales for me, tells me
of the Naval Academy Planetarium:

They take you in there - it is dark.
They show you one constellation -
just one. They say, what is that star ?
We have to learn one hundred stars.

Ny Alesund

This is the end of the world.
Here, the last shop, the last
telephone. In Pyramiden,
Longyearbyen, they said,
North of here there is nothing,
nothing but Ny Alesund, and its scientists.

And at Ny Alesund there is, indeed, nothing
but North itself.

In the winter, bears come from the hills
grey in our arclights, overturn
the skips, eat our sweet
garbage. We hear the frenzy
in the dog-pens, watch
from first storey windows.

Afterwards, in their excrement we find
aluminium foil, shreds of tin cans;
once, the year the tourists
died, the zip of a cagoul
of German manufacture.

In Ny Alesund, we celebrate
our latitude, display it
on mugs, sweatshirts,
78° 56' North.

Two hundred metres from the pier,
the post office. Four hundred metres
from the pier, wilderness.
You are forbidden to leave Ny Alesund
unless you bear a firearm,
minimum 7.62 calibre.

The government posted an inspector here.
Each night he drank, then he stole

a car, drove round and round the village.
A helicopter had to come for him
from Barentsburg: pilots, aviation fuel,
two thousand dollars. They made him pay for it,
then charged him with theft, misuse
of government property, and professional
misconduct. Technically he had committed
no traffic offence as there are no roads here
that meet international definitions.

From Ny Alesund, there are only two
directions: the pole, and failure.
We come after those who follow
the explorers, coming as far
as they can after their sons,
fathers. Frost welds their crucifixes
to the list of etched and absent names.
The marble busts of Amundsen
and Nobile stand at the edge of town, look out
on nothing. A plaque:
A Tutti Gli Esploratori Polari
di Ogni Tempo e Ogni Nazione

In the winter, the helicopter comes
once a fortnight, bringing newspapers
from Tromso, scientists, marmalade.
When the weather is bad it does
not come, and in the winter the weather
is usually bad. It is advisable to bring your own
supplies of anything you may need.

Our two hours has expired; we must go
North. The harbour master
talks to the crew in Russian, flirts
in Norwegian with the officers,
waves us off. Above her office
she has written a sign.

Ny Alesund. 78° 56' North.

Polar Hotel

Welcome to the United Nations Conference
on the Preservation of Arctic Mammals!
Main course whale steak in garlic sauce.

Ocean currents are concentrating pollutants
in arctic waters to toxic strength.
Tonight, Bar Special: Arctic Cocktails!
White rum and vodka with glacier ice.

Many of you have travelled here to see a Polar bear.
Svalbard has the highest quantity
of bears in Europe. If a bear arrives,
you must leave immediately.

Guests are advised not to exit the hotel
without a firearm which can be hired locally.
It is prohibited to carry loaded weapons within
dining room, bedrooms or sauna area.

Carry this guide with you at all times.
Bears may be hungry or curious.
A curious bear will be a threat
only if it regards you as a food source.
Do not run from a curious bear.

If a bear comes near you, shout
and wave your arms. This may scare
a curious bear, but is ineffective
against a hungry bear. In the spring
all bears are hungry. Do not run. Shoot flares.

Do not shoot flares behind the bear
as this may prompt an attack.

If a bear comes within a hundred metres
take off items of clothing and throw them.
This may delay a curious bear.

If the bear comes within fifty metres, do not run.
The bear is a protected species.
Shoot it repeatedly in the chest area.

Below fifty metres chance of survival
is low. The bear can travel at speeds
of up to 50km / hr so running
will not be effective.

Avoid all intimate contact
with wild animals.The island
is a rabies infested area.

Wildlife is protected by international treaty.
Shooting of bears is a criminal matter
and will be investigated by the authorities.
Failure to report may lead to imprisonment.
Note the sex of bear and if possible its weight.

In the event of death of persons
this must be reported to the Governor
during working hours.

Ytrenorskoya

First we buried them
hacking holes in the frozen topsoil
but they came back to us, thrust up
by the rising ice, shouldering aside our crosses,
pushing plank coffins through the mud.

Then we built cairns, till in the long dark
when the ice thickens and the seals are few,
the bears came, scattering the stones
and after them the white foxes
and screaming gulls, bearing
scraps of winding sheet and skin.

Now in the spring we do
as the Dutch do, sailing to Ytrenorskoya
at the archipelago's edge, our cargo,
children, white in their stiff shrouds.

Through the winter till the ice melts
they wait their laying out, the air too pure
to rot them, and on Ytrenorskoya, wreathed
in mist and incense, the priest says the good words
above the pit, and sailors with iron spars
lever boulders onto them.

Here we bring those who have died
of fever, those with lungs burnt
by thirty degrees of frost,
those who ate polar bear liver
and the parasitic worm that breeds there,
those who drowned when the Royal Navy
sank seven whalers in the Sjorje fjord.

There is one point of landing for our boats,
one point of departure. And once each spring
we see between the clumps of stone
patches of brilliant moss, the red lichen
that grows now only on this island.

Life Long Learning

It's a game. Today, she's brought another favour
I can do for her, some essay she needs me
to tighten up a little. The black gossard
under the white blouse, the lipstick, the little
skirt. Her enormous eyes that rare shade
falling between blue and purple, the bruised
violet of deep water, swollen clouds,
the hard dark glossy sheen of folded wings
on insects in long grass. The only eyes ever
to be that colour. She's playing with her
hair. *It's so hot in here!* She has the trick
of gazing round the room, tormenting
restless buttons in her fingers. She holds me
in her confidence, a sort of trophy, insatiable
audience for her tales of flirting with disaster.

She eats chocolate one bite at a time, flicking glances
at me, licks her fingers clean, leaving me tongue-
tied, calls me *sugar daddy.* All's fair. She's just picked up
her party photos, lets me watch her
leaf through them, flashing that lacy dress,
her snogging her best friend: *Sometimes we pretend*
we're lesbians? It drives men wild
In every one, her eyes invite the lens.
I've got to make the money,
somehow. I thought of escort work. I'm good
at giving people what they they want.
Her gaze swallows me up. *What do you think?*

I thought, that afternoon, of the Adelphi
ballroom; of two girls, eighteen, nineteen,
in New Look party wear, stretching
thin lipstick smiles, pinching with scarlet nails
bright orange cocktails: scared, excited eyes
glancing off a pair of balding men, their red fat
hands fingering their shorts, drinking
in cleavage, mouths, crossed thighs.

All this comes back, in that breathless pause
while Lauren from La Femme: *For any Taste,*
any Occasion, puts me on hold, gets back,
Of course, sir, I can do that for you.
Would you like blue or brown?

Jill

Lots of guys say that. Her lopsided smile
pulls one lip corner down, exposing a pink twist
of flesh, the angry bloodsore on a glimpse
of gum. *They all ask if I'm a model.* Her nails,
pearl varnished, lift the fivers to the light,
pick each silver strip. In the driving mirror
her cheeks are faintly specked with glitter
dust, her swollen pupils hold green pools
of darkness like a spell. - *But they're wrong,*
I'm not pretty. She shrugs out of the bra,
pulls back bony shoulders, one nipple
turned in, shy, the hollow of her stomach
pale as lilies. This close, her breath tastes
of cigarettes and rain, her hair's a black cascade,
thick, soft, as cat's fur in my hands.
I've got a nice mouth, though.
Guys'll pay a lot for a good mouth. Anyway -
As I put my hands on her, her eyes turn blank.
Somewhere in the dark, behind the broken
saplings, tattered plastic bags, a fractured moon
is rising, snowdrops pierce the skin
of January soil like needles, rooks flutter
to their roosts around the park. I grow
to fill her hand, her small touch
cold as the streets; tight, numb, determined
as a child's around an icicle. She squeezes,
bites her tongue, her nails, half luminous,
blurring to a fairy gleam, flinches as her face
is splashed by passing headlights, swallows
hard, half-smiles - *we're all pretty in the dark.*

Lorrayne

Her life is full of miracles. *Things happen,*
and it's, like, I've dreamed them before ?
Last week she found a DVD player
among the binbags on her street. *It works.*
Honest? Her horoscope warns when to go out,
black cats which streets not to walk.
It's intuition? There's some cars
you just don't get into, you know ?

I've pulled in out of sight, among the rubbish,
squares of shattered glass, the site
of some old factory, a house.
Will you do my cards for me, after?
The wipers flog the dark, then die,
folded on each other. She's painted now
by every fleeting light, her arms thin mirrors
to the orange radiance of halogen. The beams
of distant cars sweep her pale back.
Could you make it thirty-five?
I've got to pay the rent. The handbrake
warning light – a single angry
exclamation mark - bleeds onto her palm.
Her hair is wet as rags.
My boobs are better now – see?
Tattooed on one small breast, a tiny heart
in red. *I smell alright, don't I?*
Between her thighs her flesh
starves into hollow curves. As she moves
my hands clasp three tight ribs
in each cold span.
It's only girl smell, isn't it?

Afterwards I lay for her, crowded
on the seat, the Queen of Rods, the High Priestess.
Don't worry, I won't touch them.
They're good cards, aren't they?
As I drive back she takes my sweets,

tells me of the shoes she's seen for twenty pounds
in TJ Hughes; the guy who paid her
to smear her feet with spit and walk on him;
her friend Sam, raped by two men in an Audi.
Her mum. Her eyes meet mine, dead level
as she talks. When she gets out she says,
You take care now. There's bad girls
out here, all kinds.

Can I help you?

Kitty and Co   Pussy Cats
Feline Girls   Pink Katz
Fantasia   Obsessions   Dreams
Passions   Affinity   Close Encounters
Lolita's   Mermaids   Whispers
Fingertips   Velvet Touch
The Vixen's Den   Babes in the Wood
Sindarellas   Black Velvet   Sensations
Touch of Class   Rachael Rachael
Marcia's   Fiona's   Bunny Girls
Cartier Girls   Diamonds   Oriental Princess
Venus   Cleopatra's   Pharoah's
Jezebels   Little Devils   Babylon Girls
Taboo   Temptation   Multitude of Sins
Garden of Eden   Fallen Angels
Heaven Scent   Devotions   Paradise
The Sanctuary   Sacred Rose
Alpha   Omega   Enigma
Mystique   Aquarius   Northern Star
Blue Ice   Superstars   Ladybirds
Honeys   Swallows   Pure Pleasures
Temporarily Yours   Discretion
Kiss   La Femme   Bliss

Mistress Tanya

Sorry, darling. Her eyes are bloodshot.
Fucking maid should be here. She's tiny:
four foot ten, hair scraped back, acne,
shell suit. *You been waiting long?*
Holding her breakfast in sagging chip paper.
Behind, her cab reverses, pulls away
into the morning traffic. *Can you hold this, babes?*
I fumble with it, smearing warm ketchup
on my hands, wipe it on my coat, and she susses me
in one swift look: harmless.
Let's get inside, babes.

Sensations Massage. It's freezing, dark, stinks
of cigarettes and Pine Fresh Glade. In the lounge
a desk, a sofa worn to the threads, the phone,
bleeping. She plays the message: *Sorry Hayley*
friggin baby sitter again. Can you open up?

She locks the door. *Give me a minute, babes.*
You want a coffee there's no milk?
You don't mind me having a bite first?
Fucking head's killing me. I was that pissed last night
honest to God, my head in the frigging toilet,
what was you after, hon, bit of oral?
Just be a minute babes.

She leaves the door open, speaks
through the toilet's splash and gurgle,
You want the Kinky stuff ?
I do all the domination and that.
By the phone's a pack of Regal, the rota
stained with coffee, and the script
JORDAN, 34 Double D, Blonde, blue eyes,
former model, a fabulous figure
and a filthy mind. O and A levels.
Satisfaction guaranteed.
MISTRESS TANYA, for your darkest
fantasies. Tall, slim, brown eyes,
offers bondage, S/M, domination
Your pain is her pleasure.

She stands in the loo door, naked, her breasts
small, tired, cheeks pitted with hollows,
holding a hairbrush and a cigarette. *You want*
the uniform and that? She takes a drag, exhales,
arranges pots, brushes, eyeliner, on the shelf.
Her calves are knotted with bruised veins.
Got no whip I'm sorry. Friggin Denise
gone off with it. Boyfriend likes all that.
She pulls the bobble out and hair
floods around her shoulders, glossy, dark. She scours
it till it shines, reaches for foundation, blusher.

Outside buses heave by, a truck. Frost
fringes the blacked out window, swirled to patterns
of ferns and curling leaves. In the mirror
a new face appears, skin gentled
into smoothness, pale as chalk,
svelte cheek bones. The eyes are startling,
bright, the lashes stark. Her mouth scarlet.

I'll need your money first hon?
From a locker she reaches the black corset
in PVC, dewed with condensation. She pulls it on,
shivers, tugs the laces till it blunts her nipples,
creases across her back. Takes out
the boots, dagger-heeled, longer than her arms.
A soft gleam chases over them.
The zips' steel snarl glints in the light.

Give me a hand here, babes?
As she balances I kneel on the cold floor,
the spikes of five inch heels punish my palms.
I feel her small toes pushing deep inside
the leather, and then she's in, tight, snug,
the zips' purr rising to a squeal. She stamps,
stands tall, looks down on me, so close
my shallow breathing mists the glossy mirror
of her thigh, crushes her cigarette, says

What am I going to do
with you, babes?

Speaking in Tongues

Are you sure, Fiona asks, you're not a priest? Ten minutes left
before her next, and she lies on her back, knees bent up, her red hair
fanned across the lilac sheet, dabbing her chest with a wet wipe.
I pour her a warm coke. Outside it's eighty-eight degrees; inside,
the fan grinds back and forth. From one wall come the usual sounds,

from the other, Caprice, ten hours into a twelve hour shift, saying,
trust me, it happens all the time. Have it your way, Fiona says,
I've been around too long. They come in here around Lent,
the young ones, before they take their vows. And then I see them after.

Two pigeons flurry at the skylight, fall exhausted and Caprice
is trying again when Fiona says, You know this place was haunted?
Lights coming on and off, ashtrays flying round. All that stuff. Bloody
punter, of course. Dead and nowhere better to hang around than here
the bastard. Didn't bother me. I says, *if you can move plates about,*
why don't you do the bloody washing up? But the wee girlies
were getting frightened. Voices. Touching their hair. And then it's bad

for business. So there's this one guy - one of my regulars. I had a feeling
about him. I didn't ask, cause then it makes it awkward. I just says
to him, *I've got this problem. Now could you maybe do something,*
just as a favour ? Looks that damn surprised, I tell you.
Then all serious, he says *I'll need to be alone, Fiona.*
She passes me some tissue, sips her coke, and I see

him standing in this room, naked, his right hand lifted, quartering
the air. His breath slowing, the pulse of the fan, the cars outside, all
slowing, beginning the Liturgy of Deliverance and as he speaks
something growing present, clawing at his nerves, a burden in the air
an outline at the edge of vision, the muscles in his neck
tensing, sweat glistening on his temples, running in the hollow
of his spine and then, unasked, his throat convulsing saliva

flooding in his mouth and breaking in the room the tongue
of angels, harsh with the arid rhythms of the desert
the air opening to his words the way that eggshell opens for a bird
or snake. His palms scorching and all this, the bed,
the table with its folded towels, the plate of Durex, Asda talc, blazing
holy, their colours scalding, the light of every thing awoken, and then the peace

of nothing, the carpet, walls, fading to dullness, and him standing
here, the air chilling on his skin, the damp prints of his feet, his hair
matted, limp, and outside the shrill summons
of the pelican lights on Dundas street.

Right enough, Fiona says, he did the job. Not that I'm religious -
Christmas and weddings, me. But I could tell, he'd cleared it out.
I owe you, I says to him and then he says to me *Fiona, you realise,*
he says, *I'm really sorry, hen. I can't come back here now.*

Bianca

Her smile lights up the lounge. She says
 - thanks for asking, though. The weird thing is
they're queuing up for me. Yesterday
I did fourteen. How mad is that?

She's slumped back in her chair, her feet up,
red wonderbra, black knickers,
scraping a stiletto on the coffee table. - It's all so weird.
I'm lying there on Morag's floor, nothing to wear
but what I had in casualty and frigging Fiona
phones me up. *The punters are all asking*
for you. As if, I said. Bye. And then Wednesday
she rings again. *Lucky oral's your speciality*
she says and I say I don't believe this

and I just hung up. And Thursday she's on again
I'm desperate she says *The two new girls have left,*
I caught one stealing. I'm going to have to close.
and I'm like, sorry Fiona. Then yesterday

it's like somehow she knows, my painkillers
run out, I'm staring at the walls,
and then she phones, all nice.
A time like this, you need to be where friends are.
I'll look out for you, bring you cups of tea.
Which was shit, but it gets me in, and then I'm here,
and I'm thinking, well I might as well
make something. And the first guy I do
he wants to sign it. I says what do you think I am,
the frigging visitors book?

And then there's all these regulars
who never used to book with me before, and now
they're gagging for it. *Call it a niche market,*
Fiona says. *The punters always go*
for something unusual. I tell you, keep
the crutches after, just for work. And I'm thinking,
she's serious. Itches like fuck, I'll tell you.

She leans forward, to push one red nail
into the tight slit where the heavy cast
pinches round her leg. She scratches, angry,
the white skin flushed then white again
then swollen, red, when she pulls her finger
free. Where the plaster ends
her toe-nails are painted purple.

- It's all so crazy ? And then there was this girl,
I saw her by Haymarket. Tall, like, blonde,
and she's got a limp, and I'm thinking
what happened to you and then I see
the cab driver's watching her - I mean, like *watching,*
and as she's walking down the street I see
all these guys, looking, it's like it turns them on.
It does, I'm not joking, it's so fucking weird
and then I'm thinking maybe that's why Steve
did it to me the bastard.

Homecoming

Another hour of driving, sleeping farmsteads,
jagged turns, and then this garage, its lights
an island in the dark. I pull over, step out, lost,
unsteady in the forecourt's glare, the darkness
of the mountains crowding round, the pumps beaded with rain.
The whirr and throb of deisel, the wind
filling the silence.

There's been no sign. But in the kiosk, Tunnock's Teacakes,
Mackie's milk, the Herald: *Fifth Vice Girl Murdered;*
the border elided somewhere in the night.
My way from here is mapped:
TOWN CENTRE, TOURIST ROUTE:
persistent street lamps fading in the dawn;
the moment when the sun first strokes the trees;
my road; huge skies, clouds piled in slate
and white and blue; deerfences and Dutch barns;
crows flapping from the verge; pylons ranged
for miles across the fields;
the sweet heaviness of barley in the dew.

Coed y Farden

I

Coed y Farden: three square miles where no one comes
by foot, or land-rover, for days on end :
bounded by crumbling dykes and rusting wire,
the river choked with flashflood branches;
lines of pines and spruce broken, thinned
by fifty years of storm, their fallen trunks
opening ragged glades to ash and rowan
seedlings of oak and holly: no longer
forestry plantation, not yet wild wood.

A place where silence holds
within it the surf-surge of the spruce, the mutter of water,

yet rests unbroken, its stillness
not absence of sound
but strands of quiet through which the place itself listens:

the soft pad
as drifts of needles yield under my boots;

the changing in the river's voice
as I cross its current, the way it closes back again;

the flat chime of barbed wire springing back
vibrating from post to post into the soil.

II

It's only here I know
this cleanness of the air, of pine and peat

Here under the rain, a cold stone at my back,
there whispers at the edge of thought a sense

of subtle territories of blood and scent
a cigarette smoked half a mile away,

the taint of deisel and exhaust
lingering on the track for hours
after the foresters have gone

a stillness that has me turning, sometimes
to the crow's flight before I hear it
sometimes to see nothing
visible.

Lives which compass mine
the way the buzzard's circles hold
the lesser worlds of rook and heron;

which intersect with mine only the way
the mud at dawn unites the tracks
of fox and polecat, their hunger hours apart.

III

It's only here that I acknowledge
that this is my religion,
underpinning everything, this bond
I've made with you and never spoken,
that you understand runs deeper
than any marriage, a kind of parenthood,

in which your spirit finds no rest
but still a place to venture from
and to return. A faith
whose confirmations are all ambiguous:
voices in the wind;
an empty bed: mud on the stairs;
the grit your tongue discovers
between your teeth.

It's here, in Coed y Farden, that I believe
this love, patient, unforseen, may redeem
all that is merely human, its proof
absolute discretion; the tenderness

of ordinary things: to wait
in the tired dawn and watch

for your eyes opening; to dress
the scratches on your limbs;

return you to your name.

January

Leaving the house before dawn, returning
late, my home becomes for weeks on end

a place of darkness: cold owl call greeting me
after the slam of the car door; the moment's

exhalation and relief. Then with the in-breath
frost burning in my throat; my neighbour's

woodsmoke; the silence of Sirius singing
in the branches of the ash, the world

large again. All this month I have come
to bed knowing I have achieved

nothing, nothing to save from the day
that has passed but ragged minutes

of prayer, thanks spoken and pleas
offered beneath Orion and Auriga

to spirits I cannot name. They come,
or seem to come, answering

to fire and air, teach me to find
their eyes in the blurred glimmer

of the stream I know now
only by moonlight or darkness. I hear

their voices in the swirl and clink
of the river as it thickens with ice.

Each night I have stood in mist or rain
at the same bend in the road, the same patch

of trodden mud beside the gate,
till persistence or exhaustion has worn

thin whatever ether lies between
my clumsy desires and their searing

tenderness. Until, it seems, it is they
who come between fields and stars,

summoning, and I who answer.